How to Draw
Rhode Island's
Sights and Symbols

Aileen Weintraub

The Rosen Publishing Group's
PowerKids Press™
New York

Published in 2002 by The Rosen Publishing Group, Inc.
29 East 21st Street, New York, NY 10010

First Edition

Editors: Gillian Brown, Nancy MacDonell Smith
Book Design: Kim Sonsky
Layout Design: Michael Donnellan

Illustration Credits: Jamie Grecco
Photo Credits: p. 7 © G.E. Kidder Smith/CORBIS, (inset) © Lee Snider; Lee Snider/CORBIS; p. 8 courtesy of the Rhode Island Historical Society, neg. number: RHiX3 537; p. 9 © Museum of Art, Rhode Island School of Design, bequest of Isaac C. Bates; pp. 12, 14 © One Mile Up, Inc.; p. 16 © Scott T. Smith/CORBIS; p. 18 © Raymond Gehman/CORBIS; p. 20 © Angela Hampton; Ecoscene/CORBIS; p. 22 © David H. Wells/CORBIS; p. 24 © Owen Franken/CORBIS; p. 26 © Caroline Knight; Edifice/CORBIS; p. 28 © Joseph Sohm; ChromoSohm Inc./CORBIS.

Weintraub, Aileen, 1973–
        How to draw Rhode Island's sights and symbols / Aileen Weintraub.
            p. cm. — (A kid's guide to drawing America)
        Includes index.
        Summary: This book explains how to draw some of Rhode Island's sights and symbols, including the state seal, the official flower, and Slater Mill.
        ISBN 0-8239-6096-X
        1. Emblems, State—Rhode Island—Juvenile literature   2. Rhode Island—In art—Juvenile literature   3. Drawing—Technique—Juvenile literature   [1. Emblems, State—Rhode Island   2. Rhode Island   3. Drawing—Technique] I. Title II. Series
        2002
        743'.8'99745—dc21

Manufactured in the United States of America

CONTENTS

Let's Draw Rhode Island

Rhode Island was one of the original 13 colonies. In 1636, a man named Roger Williams founded the first permanent settlement in Rhode Island. Williams had been forced to leave Massachusetts because of his religious and political beliefs. He founded Providence, the present-day capital of Rhode Island. Freedom of religion was respected in Providence.

Rhode Island was one of the first colonies to give up its allegiance to the king of Great Britain. The colonists did not like being taxed by the king. In 1775, the American Revolution (1775–1783) began. This war helped the colonies break free from English rule and become independent states. Rhode Island was granted statehood on May 29, 1790. This state soon became the birthplace of the Industrial Revolution in the United States. A man named Samuel Slater invented the water-powered cotton mill in the 1790s. The Blackstone River Valley National Heritage Corridor was set up in 1986, to celebrate Rhode Island's history. This area is made up of 24 cities and towns, including mill villages, roads, trails, and agricultural and natural landscapes from the time of the Industrial Revolution.

In this book, you will learn how to draw the sights and the symbols of Rhode Island. Each drawing starts out with a simple step. More steps are added until the picture is complete. To shade an area, tilt your pencil sideways and rub back and forth. To draw Rhode Island's sights and symbols you will need:

- A sketch pad
- An eraser
- A number 2 pencil
- A pencil sharpener

These are some of the shapes and drawing terms you need to know to draw Rhode Island's sights and symbols:

 3-D box

 Shading

Almond shape

 Squiggle

—— Horizontal line

Teardrop

Oval

Vertical line

Rectangle

Wavy line

The Ocean State

Rhode Island is the smallest state in the Union. This is why it is often called Little Rhody. The state's full name is the State of Rhode Island and Providence Plantations. Its official nickname is the Ocean State. This is because the state has more than 400 miles (644 km) of shoreline bordering the Atlantic Ocean. There are many interesting sights in the Ocean State. Touro Synagogue, in Newport, was built in 1763 and is the country's oldest synagogue. Every year people attend the Newport Jazz Festival and the Providence Art Festival. This state is also home to a very famous potato, the toy Mr. Potato Head. Sculptures of Mr. Potato Head can be seen all around the state.

No one is completely sure how Rhode Island got its name. Some think it was named for the ancient Greek island of Rhodes. Others think it was named Roodt Eyland by a Dutch explorer because of its red clay soil. *Roodt eyland* means "red island" in Dutch.

The Touro Synagogue, built in 1763, stands in Newport, Rhode Island. The synagogue is the oldest Jewish house of worship in the Americas.

Artist in Rhode Island

Edward Mitchell Bannister was an African American artist who spent his time painting pictures of the rural farmland and the beaches of Rhode Island. Bannister was born in New Brunswick, Canada, in 1828.

Edward Mitchell Bannister

He was a free black man during the time of slavery. He moved to Boston in 1848, and he settled in Rhode Island in 1869. He taught himself how to paint, because he was not allowed to go to art school with white painters. While teaching himself to paint, he held odd jobs. He worked as a cook, a hairdresser, and a photographer.

Bannister's artistic style came from French Barbizon artists. Barbizon artists were known for painting soft, moody scenes from nature. Bannister is famous for being the first African American artist to win first prize for a painting at the Philadelphia Centennial

Exposition. This was a contest where artists showed their work. He won this award in 1876, for his painting *Under the Oaks*. Bannister was one of the founders of the Providence Art Club. The painting below is called *At the Oakside Beach* and is an example of his work. He painted it in 1877 in the same style as his earlier work. He died in 1901, having produced more than 1,000 works of art.

The painting above is called *At the Oakside Beach* and measures 11 ⅞″ x 7 ⅞″ (30.1 cm x 19.7 cm). He uses shading in his paintings just like you will use shading in your drawings.

Map of Rhode Island

Map of the Continental United States

Rhode Island is one of the New England states. Massachusetts borders it to the north and the east, Connecticut to the west, and the Atlantic Ocean to the south. Narragansett Bay runs through two-thirds of the state. This bay is home to 35 islands that belong to Rhode Island. These islands vary in size. Some are just a few large rocks. Rhode Island is made up of rolling hills and valleys. The highest point in the state is Jerimoth Hill, which reaches 812 feet (247.5 m) above sea level. Rhode Island's total area is 1,231 square miles (3,189 sq km). It takes only 45 minutes to drive from one end of the state to the other.

1

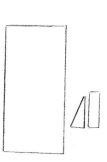

Start by drawing a large rectangle, a small triangle, and a small rectangle.

2

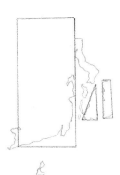

Using the shapes as a guide, draw the shape of Rhode Island.

3

Erase extra lines, and draw a circle for Newport. Add a square on Block Island.

4

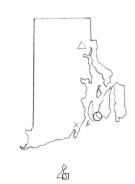

Draw a triangle for Slater Mill and an *X* for Narragansett.

5

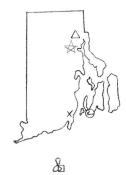

Draw a star for Providence, the capital of Rhode Island.

6

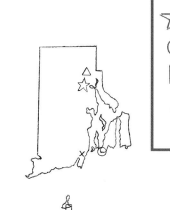

☆	Providence
○	Newport
□	Block Island
△	Slater Mill
X	Narragansett

To finish your map, make a key in the upper right corner to mark the state's points of interest.

The State Seal

Rhode Island's state seal has gone through several changes. The seal that is used today was introduced in 1647. This seal has the word "Hope" above an anchor. This is Rhode Island's state motto. It comes from Roger Williams's words to the early settlers, "Hope in the Divine." In the center of the seal is an anchor. The anchor is an important symbol for Rhode Island. This symbol is a reminder of the importance of the ocean to this state. Around the entire seal are the words "Seal of the State of Rhode Island and Providence Plantations." On the bottom of the seal is the year Rhode Island was founded, 1636.

1

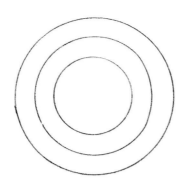

Start by drawing three circles, one inside another.

2

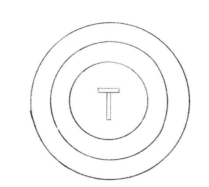

In the center, add two rectangles in the shape of a *T* for the top of the anchor.

3

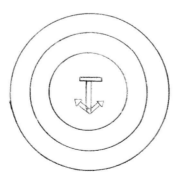

Add two more rectangles and two triangles to finish the anchor.

4

Erase extra lines, and draw the decorations around the anchor.

5

Add small triangles around the large circle.

6

Write "SEAL OF THE STATE OF RHODE ISLAND AND PROVIDENCE PLANTATIONS" and 1636 in the middle circle. Write "HOPE" in the banner. Erase the large circle.

13

The State Flag

Rhode Island's state flag has one of the most unique designs of all the flags in the Union. On the flag, a gold anchor is set against a white background. Below the anchor is a blue ribbon with the word "Hope" embroidered in gold letters. A circle of 13 stars surrounds the anchor and the state motto. The stars represent the original 13 colonies. The colors white and blue were chosen because these were the colors used in flags carried by Rhode Island's soldiers during the eighteenth and the nineteenth centuries. The original flag was adopted in 1877. This flag underwent a few changes. The one used today, with the design described above, was adopted in 1897.

1

Start by drawing a large rectangle for the flag's field.

2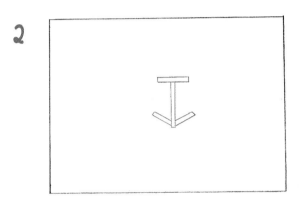

Add four rectangles in the center of the flag for the anchor.

3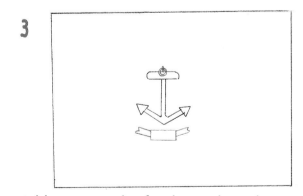

Add two triangles for the anchor's bottom and three rectangles for the banner. Then add a circle to the top of the anchor.

4

Add 13 stars around the anchor.

5

Erase extra lines. Write the word "HOPE" in the banner, and your flag is done.

15

The Violet

Rhode Island was the first of four states to choose the violet as the state flower, but it was the last state to make its choice official. In 1890, Rhode Island school commissioner Thomas Stockwell organized a vote for both the state tree and the state flower. Students voted for their favorite flower, and the violet won. It wasn't until March 11, 1968, that this choice was made official. That was when Francis Sherman, a politician and a teacher, introduced the state flower bill to Rhode Island's legislature. By that time, all the other states had official flowers.

1

Start by drawing a circle for the center of the flower.

2

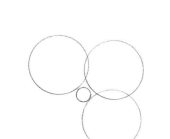

To make petals, add three circles around the center.

3

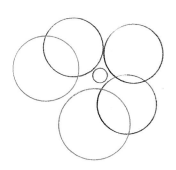

Add two larger circles for the last of the petals.

4

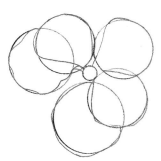

Using the circles as guides, draw the shape of the petals.

5

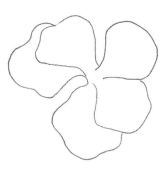

Erase extra lines.

6

Add shading and detail to your flower, and you're done.

The Red Maple

Did you know that there is always at least one red part on a red maple tree throughout the year? There are red blossoms in April, red seeds in May, crimson leaf stems during the summer, scarlet leaves in the fall, and bright red twigs and buds in the winter. In 1890,  Rhode Island school commissioner Thomas Stockwell allowed children over the age of 10 to vote for the state tree. The red maple won, but two other trees, the maple barley and the elm, were close seconds. The red maple wasn't officially adopted until 1964. This made Rhode Island one of the last states to adopt a state tree.

1

Start by drawing a small rectangle for the tree trunk.

2

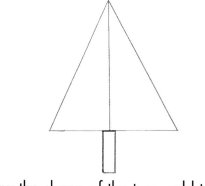

To draw the shape of the tree, add two large triangles over the thin rectangle.

3

Using the triangle as a guide, draw branches from the center of the triangle.

4

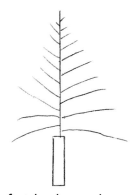

Once you've finished your branches, erase the large triangle.

5

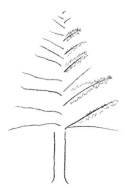

Erase the center line and draw little M shapes for the leaf clusters around the branches.

6

Add detail and shading. Your tree is complete.

The Rhode Island Red

   Would you believe that the smallest state has the largest state bird? The Rhode Island Red was not the state's first choice to be the state bird. Mrs. J. Howard Pember, chairperson of the State Federation division of conservation and natural resources, began campaigning for a Rhode Island state bird in 1931. The bobwhite won the most votes, followed closely by the osprey. Both choices were submitted to the state legislature, but neither was chosen. In 1954, the Audubon Society of Rhode Island held a new vote for the state bird. This time the Rhode Island Red, a type of chicken, won the most votes. The Rhode Island Red was first bred in Little Compton, Rhode Island, in 1854.

1

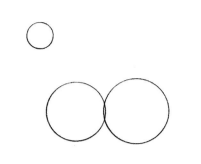

Start by drawing three circles for the rough shape of the bird. The smallest circle is for the head, and the two larger circles are for the body.

2

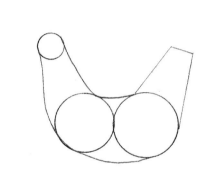

Connect your circles to form the shape of the bird's body, and add a rectangle for the tail.

3

Use wavy lines to round the shape of the tail. Erase extra lines and smudges. Add a triangle-shaped beak with an oval under it.

4

Erase extra lines, and add two curvy triangles for legs. Draw in the wing shape. You can also add an eye.

5

Erase extra lines. Draw the legs and the feet. Add a triangle shape to the top of the head.

6

Add shading and detail to your bird, and you're done. Smudge your lines to make the shading more effective.

Slater Mill

In 1789, an Englishman named Samuel Slater came to America. In England Slater had worked as a laborer in a textile mill. He took the knowledge he had learned about mills in England and opened America's first water-powered cotton mill on the Blackstone River in Pawtucket, Rhode Island. The machinery turned raw cotton into cloth very quickly. After the success of Slater Mill, many other mills opened along the river and throughout the state. The opening of these mills was the beginning of the Industrial Revolution in the United States. Today Slater Mill is a museum dedicated to American industry. Samuel Slater has gone down in history as the founder of the American Industrial Revolution.

1

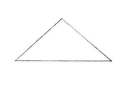

Start by drawing a large triangle and a small triangle for the roofs.

2

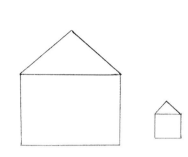

Add two rectangles for the building fronts.

3

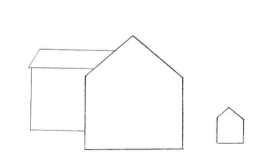

Erase extra lines, and add two more rectangles for the building's wing.

4

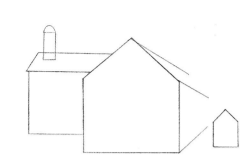

Add a small rectangle and a half circle for the peak. Add three slanted lines to give the building depth.

5

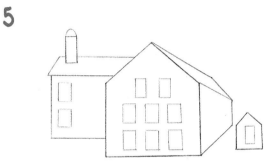

Erase extra lines. Connect the rear of the house, and then add windows using rectangles.

6

Add shading and detail to your building, and you're done. You can also smudge your lines to make the shading more effective.

The Quahog

On July 1, 1987, the quahog became Rhode Island's official state shell. The quahog is a hard-shell clam that was once used by Native Americans as wampum. Wampum were beads made from the clam's shell and used as money. The Native Americans called the quahog *poquauhock*. Today Rhode Island is known as quahog country, because so many of these clams are caught in the state. Quahogs are dark in color and live along Rhode Island's shorelines. They bury themselves deep in the sand or the mud. This makes searching for quahogs dirty work. A quahog can live up to 60 years if fishermen or natural predators, such as birds, don't catch it.

1

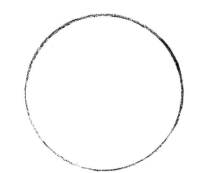

Start by drawing a circle as a guide.

2

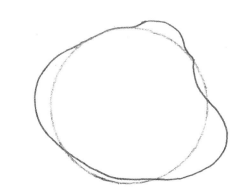

Use the circle as a center, and draw the shape of the shell.

3

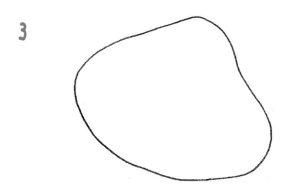

Erase extra lines.

4

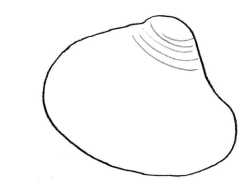

Start drawing thin lines across the shell.

5

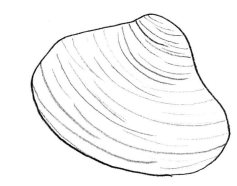

Finish drawing the lines on the shell, and erase any smudges.

6

Add shading, and you're done. To make the shading more effective, smudge your lines

The Marble House

Newport, Rhode Island, is filled with beautiful mansions built during the last three centuries. The Marble House was built in 1892 as a summer home for Mr. and Mrs. William K. Vanderbilt, a rich railroad businessman and his wife. The time period during which this house was built is known as the Gilded Age. This was a time when wealthy and powerful people built expensive homes and collected great works of art. The Marble House is made up of 500,000 cubic feet (14,158 m^3) of marble. When the house was finished, Mr. Vanderbilt gave it to his wife as a birthday present. Today tourists can visit the house and can rediscover part of America's history.

1

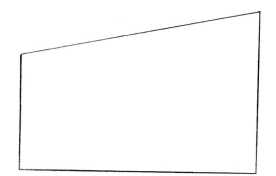

Start by drawing a large, slanted rectangle.

2

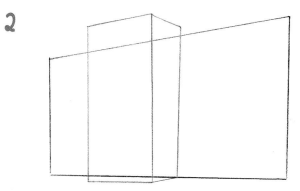

Add two rectangles for the building's entrance.

3

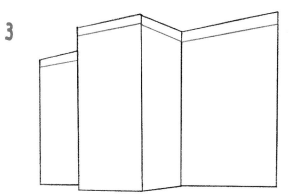

Erase extra lines, and add four thin rectangles on the roof.

4

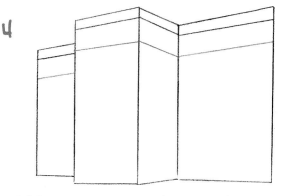

Add four more rectangles near the top of the building.

5

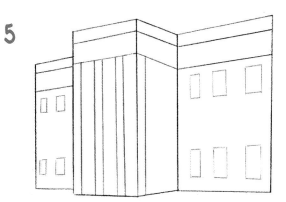

Add four columns using thin, vertical rectangles, and draw the windows.

6

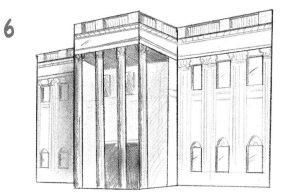

Add shading and detail to your building, and you're done. Smudging your lines can make the shading more effective.

27

Rhode Island's Capitol

On September 16, 1895, construction began on Rhode Island's state capitol. Charles McKim, an architect from New York, designed the building. It was completed on June 11, 1904. The capitol building is made of white Georgia marble. It has the second-largest unsupported marble dome in the world. The largest is the dome on Saint Peter's Church in Rome, Italy. Rhode Island's capitol contains important historical artifacts, including the Gettysburg gun. This gun was used during the Civil War (1861–1865) at the Battle of Gettysburg. Set into the floor inside the building is a brass replica of the Rhode Island state seal. There are many different types of artwork in the building, including murals of the first settlers of Rhode Island.

1

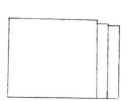

Start by drawing three rectangles for the building's wings.

2

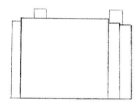

Add three more rectangles.

3

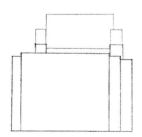

Add four more rectangles for the bases of the domes.

4

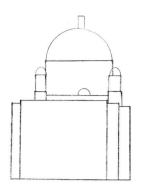

Add four half circles for the domes and a small rectangle on the large center dome.

5

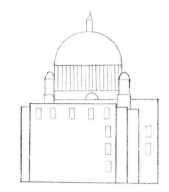

Erase extra lines, and add two more lines to complete the building. Draw in columns and windows with rectangles.

6

Finish the windows. Add shading and detail to your building, and you're done. You can also smudge your lines to make the shading more effective.

Rhode Island State Facts

Statehood	May 29, 1790, 13th state
Area	1,231 square miles (3,189 sq km)
Population	988,000
Capital	Providence, population, 152,600
Most Populated City	Providence
Industries	Health services, tourism, textiles, metal products
Agriculture	Vegetables, dairy products, eggs
Bird	Rhode Island Red
Flower	Violet
Mineral	Bowenite
Motto	Hope
Shell	Quahog
Song	"Rhode Island"
Stone	Cumberlandite
Tree	Red maple

Glossary

allegiance (uh-LEE-jents) Support of a country, group, or cause.

anchor (AN-ker) A device made of metal attached to a ship by a cable and cast overboard to hold the ship in place.

architect (AR-kih-tekt) Someone who designs buildings.

artifacts (AR-tih-fakts) Objects created and produced by humans.

centennial (sen-TEH-nee-uhl) Relating to a hundredth anniversary.

divine (dih-VYN) Of or relating to God.

exposition (ek-spuh-ZIH-shun) A public show.

federation (feh-duh-RAY-shun) A group of organizations.

founders (FOWND-erz) People who bring a group or a company into being.

gilded (GILD-ed) Covered with gold.

industrial revolution (in-DUS-tree-ul reh-vuh-LOO-shun) A time in history when power-driven machines were first used to produce goods in large quantities.

landscapes (LAND-skayps) Views of scenery on land.

legislature (LEH-jihs-lay-cher) A body of people that has the power to make or pass laws.

moody (MOOD-ee) Dark and gloomy.

murals (MYUR-ulz) Pictures painted on walls or ceilings. A mural usually covers most of a wall.

predators (PREH-duh-terz) Animals that kill other animals for food.

replica (REH-plih-kuh) A copy.

resources (REE-sors-ez) Supplies or sources of energy or useful materials.

synagogue (SIH-nih-gog) A place of worship for Jewish people.

textile (TEK-styl) Woven fabric or cloth.

unique (yoo-NEEK) Being one of a kind.

Index

Web Sites

To find out more about Rhode Island, check out these Web sites:
http://visitrhodeisland.com
www.state.ri.us